Mints

by Tameron Dennis
illustrated by Kate Flanagan

Core Decodable 13

McGraw Hill Education

Bothell, WA • Chicago, IL • Columbus, OH • New York, NY

MHEonline.com

Send all inquiries to:
McGraw-Hill Education
8787 Orion Place
Columbus, OH 43240

ISBN: 978-0-02-145313-9
MHID: 0-02-145313-6

Printed in the United States of America.

7 8 9 LCR 25 24 23

Tim had a tin can.

The tin can had mints in it.

Tim had a mint.

Tim hid it in a hand.

Did Sid see it?

"Sit, Sid," said Tim.

Sid sat.

Sid had a mint!

Tim had a mint.

Tim hid it in a hand.

Did Tam see it?

"Stand, Tam," said Tim.

Tam did stand.

Tam and Sid had a mint!